Earth Deities & Other Rhythmic Masques by Bliss Carman

Co-Authored by Mary Perry King

William Bliss Carman was born in Fredericton, in New Brunswick on April 15th 1861. He was educated at Fredericton Collegiate School before moving to the University of New Brunswick, obtaining his B.A. there in 1881. As is common with so many writers his first published piece was for the University magazine and for Carman that was in 1879.

After several years editing various magazines and periodicals Carman first published a poetry volume in 1893 with Low Tide on Grand Pré. There was no Canadian company prepared to publish and when an American company did so it went bankrupt.

The following year was decidedly better. His partnership with the American poet Richard Hovey had given birth to Songs of Vagabondia. It was an immediate success.

That success prompted the Boston firm, Stone & Kimball, to reissue Low Tide on Grand Pré and to hire Carman as the editor of its literary journal, The Chapbook.

Carman brought out, in 1895, Behind the Arras, a somewhat more serious and philosophical work centered on the premise of a long meditation, using the speaker's house and its many rooms, as a symbol of life and the choices to be made.

In 1896 Carman met Mrs Mary Perry King, who rapidly became patron, adviser and sometime lover. She also became his writing collaborator on two verse dramas.

In 1897 Carman published Ballad of Lost Haven, and in 1898, By the Aurelian Wall, the title poem itself was an elegy to John Keats and the book was a collection of formal elegies.

As the century turned Carman was hard at work on a five-volume set of poetry "Pans Pipes". The excellence of a number of these poems did much to install Carman as the most noted of Canadian Poets and eventually their own Poet Laureate.

In 1912 the final work in the Vagabondia series was published. Richard Hovey had died in 1900 and so this last work was purely Carman's. It has a distinct elegiac tone as if remembering the past works themselves.

On October 28th, 1921 Carman was honored by the newly-formed Canadian Authors' Association where he was crowned Canada's Poet Laureate with a wreath of maple leaves.

William Bliss Carman died of a brain hemorrhage at the age of 68 in New Canaan on the 8th June, 1929.

Index of Contents

THE DANCE DIURNAL

PERSONS IN THE DANCE
A SIBYL, who chants the Prologue.
Voices off Scene.
NIGHT.
DAY.
SHINE, son of Day.
SHADOW, daughter of Night.

A small wild valley among majestic hills.
Dim purple shadows break in wooded crests,
Where lonely peaks support the arch of sky, —
An amphitheatre canopied with stars.
Above the waiting valley's lilied floor,
Just clear of the invading oak and pine,
The low outcropping of a granite ledge
Breaks through the soil knee-high and ringed with fern,
A rocky islet in the waving grass.

To this still outpost in the wilderness,
Slow-moving, rapt in thought, a Sibyl comes,
And halts to stand at gaze across the scene, —
Veiled in the purple gray of forest boughs,
A heroic figure, tall and grave, and dim
Save for the glowing eyes as dark as earth,
And voice reverberant as a haunted reed.

There in prophetic vision of the dusk,
She who has pondered on the scroll of life,
And looked upon the hour-glass of the years
Running away its glittering living sands
That shall not cease while sun and stars endure,
Foresees the gladdening of the dawn and chants,
Accompanied by voices of the Dusk,
The prologue of the Dance of Night and Day.
Their chorus rises through the changing Light,
And Night, in purplish blue with stars of gold,
Is dimly seen to cross the glade and wait
Beside the exit to the West, while Day

Enters with tranquil power in gleaming gray.
Night turns. They meet and dance, cross and recross,
With rhythmic interchange of come and go,
As vague as the procedure of a dream.

Then enters from the East in sunlit gold
Immortal Shine. And Shadow from the side
Of vanishing Night emerges suddenly
And runs to meet him in her lilac robe.
These youthful shapes of joy and tenderness,
With all the ecstasy of kindling life,
Dance the bright dance of Noon, while Day looks on,
A patient sentinel among the trees.

As Day moves Westward, in the lessening light
Shine wearies and his ardent dancing flags,
Surrendering in a last caress. In the East
Night reappears; and straightway tarrying Day
And Shine and Shadow with returning Night
Tread the soft dance of twilight and of dew.
Then in the final tableau of the dusk,
Shine turns away to thread the Western wood,
And where Day with remembering eyes looks back,
Eastward moves Night with Shadow on her breast.
Then rising with a rapt and lonely chant,
The Sibyl slowly passes from the scene.

THE SIBYL (Down left front while action goes on up stage.)

(**NIGHT** moves slowly across stage.)

Here blue-robed and sovereign Night,
Sandalled with mysterious might,

Shrouded in her star-sown veil,
Passes where the moon grows pale,

Going slowly down the west
On her immemorial quest.

(**DAY** enters and approaches **NIGHT**.)

Then upon the Road of Years
Day unheralded appears,

Confident master of the way,
Strong, inscrutable, and gray,

With the light of Paradise
In his undefeated eyes.

Witching Night in her retreat
Tarries on reluctant feet,

Tenderly, for by these two
Heaven and earth are made anew.

(They Dance.)

Not an atom but must sway
To the rhythm of Night and Day.

(Dawn lights appear and change)

New-born colors wake and stir,
Light and sheer as gossamer,

Over meadow, stream, and grove,
Lilac, lavender, and mauve.

Flushing crimsons flood and change
O'er the summits range on range,

As with magic to and fro
The diurnal dancers go,

Moving in a slow pavane
Older than the breed of man.

(Light grows to a golden glow centring where **SHINE** enters)

Then below the paling stars
Time lets down the glowing bars

From the portal of the East,
And a thousand spears released

Usher in the Son of Day,
On his shining princely way.
(Enter SHINE.)
Quick to meet him from the West,
Stealing from her mother's breast,

(Enter **SHADOW**.)

Shadow in smoke-pale attire

Flutters 'neath his cloak of fire.

(**NIGHT** slowly exits.)

O departing Night and kind,
Thou must ever leave behind

Lovely Shadow here to play
With the radiant child of Day!

(**DAY** remains calmly on scene, moving imperceptibly toward exit.)

And what dancers are these two,
Shine and Shadow, gold and blue!

He is straighter than a reed;
She is light as thistle seed.

Where he moves on peak or hollow,
Unreluctant she will follow.

All along the river's hem
Golden ripples dance with them,

While they lead the racing hours
Down the aisles of nodding flowers.

Through the forest glad and green
Lightly lilts their baladine.

He is reckless in his pride,
As she dances by his side.

Ah, but he must fail at length,
In his glory and his strength,

Like the passing race of men,
While she grows but greater then,

Bending all her beauty o'er him
In the twilight to adore him!

(Re-enter **NIGHT**)

Now the star of evening burns
And the grave-eyed Night returns,

To rejoin departing Day;

Shine and Shadow still delay;

And they tread the saraband
Of the twilight hand in hand,

(Dance of four.)

Weaving figures in the dusk
Redolent of rose and musk.

But across the Western hill
Shine must pass, a wanderer still,

(Exit **SHINE**)

Where Day in a little while
Follows with unwearying smile,

(Exit **DAY**)

As soft Shadow sinks from sight
On the dreamful heart of Night.

(**NIGHT** and **SHADOW** begin their exit together as slowly as possible)

So I too must take my way
Down the road of Night and Day,

With the music in my ears
Of the dancing of the spheres.

(**THE SIBYL** makes her exit, leaving **NIGHT** and **SHADOW** still moving slowly on their course.

CURTAIN

EARTH DEITIES

PERSONS IN THE MASQUE
A STUDENT
VERTUMNUS
IRIS
SYRINX
FAUNA
PSYCHE
BEROE
CERES

BACCHANTE
POMONA
DAPHNE

An open place at the foot of a wooded hill on a spring morning. The trees are in their young green. The wild cherry is in blossom. At the back of the glade, just clear of the circling wood, is a large square granite bowlder, curiously shaped like an ancient altar, and resting upon an outcropping ledge which forms a rude step around its base. It is daybreak, with the first haze of summer heat in the air. A wandering student enters. In presenting the masque, **THE STUDENT**, if desired, may speak all the lines of all the characters, interpreting their motion. There is a musical overture, and music throughout the action and lines of the Deities, as well as through the lines descriptive of those Deities for whom **THE STUDENT** speaks the lines. The lines of **SYRINX** and **CERES** may be sung or spoken by the characters themselves as they move. **BEROE's** lines may be sung or spoken by sea voices just off scene. **POMONA'S** lines may be sung partly by herself and partly by a dancing chorus of harvesters. **DAPHNE's** lines may be sung by two nymphs observing her flight.

THE STUDENT
I have come by the green and winding road
That leads from the town to the gods' abode,—

To the ancient shadowy place apart,
Where spring is born in the woodland's heart,

And over and over the ages through
The spirit of joy is made anew.

O world of glory and toil and gleam,
Made out of passion and dust and dream!

On the gladsome quest by my student vow,
I am come to this threshold of beauty now,

Where Nature sits with inscrutable eyes
Guarding her temple of mysteries.

Who knows but the magical master key,
As Plotinus taught, may be ecstasy,

And led by the sheer elation of love
And the intuitions we cannot prove,—

We may pass in a moment fleet and fine
Into the realm of the divine!

In such a grove when the world was young
Great hymns to the god of the wood were sung.

And worshippers in procession came

With garlands and pipes to praise his name,

Before ever the world grew sad and cold,
When beauty its eloquent story told

In movement and rhythm and color and line,
Where sense could interpret and heart divine

The hidden purpose, the ceaseless power,
Enhancing the fair world hour by hour.

Is it so idle to believe
That unfearing rapture may perceive,

Where the wonder rests on river and tree,
The form and features of deity?

To the doubt-free soul even now and here
What radiant presence might appear,

Living and warm, in the very guise
It wore in the glad young centuries!

This old gray stone might almost be
The altar of some divinity.

Behold, I come with gifts in hand,
As ancient usages demand,

And wreathe the stone and lift the prayer
That shall the suppliant's faith declare.

O Spirits of Earth, will ye not draw near,
If the gift be clean and the heart sincere?

Come forth in loveliness and power
And touch with glory the present hour!

VERTUMNUS appears among the trees on the rising ground, above the altar, and as he speaks, descends and lays a hand upon a corner of the stone. At his approach **THE STUDENT** seeks to conceal himself behind a tree.

VERTUMNUS
Vertumnus am I, of the turning year.
I wake in the valleys, and spring draws near.

I sweep in the veils of purple rain
Where the woodland pomps come back again.

When the blackbird shows his scarlet wing,
And all the watery marshes ring,

I lift the chorus near and far
Through violet eves to the yellow star.

I am the ardor of light and sun,
For me the sap and the well-springs run.

I sweeten the honey for murmuring bees
In the golden blooms of the willow trees.

I fill the mellow breast of earth
With fire that brings all fruits to birth.

The sweet wild cherry, the budding vine,
And the seed in the garden ground are mine.

Where'er through the woodland ways I tread,
The answering windflower lifts its head;

I look to the orchard boughs, and lo,
They break into blossom white as snow.

For all my earthlings are dear to me,.
And gay in their kinship with deity.

He turns and disappears among the trees.
THE STUDENT (reappearing)
Ah, youth everlasting, pass not so
From the world of shadows! Let me know

The secret of thy perennial power
Bringing the ardors of life to flower!

Here under heaven's tent of blue
Teach me earth's sorceries one day through!

Here to the song of the morning stream,
While leaves play softly and meadows dream,

The south wind signals, the shadows change,
The dawn-lights shimmer, the white clouds range,

As though to usher upon the scene
Of all this magic—its very queen.

(A play of changing lights marks the approach of **IRIS**.)

How well I know in the heart's quick way
What thy moving loveliness means to say!

Through the hush of speech, the ebb and flow
Of sense and feeling come and go.

As the lift and swing of the moving sea
Break into audible harmony,

So every stir of thy beauty sings
Unspoken and ineffable things.

IRIS appears from the right, enveloped in a swirl of mist.

IRIS
A dweller among the hill-tops,
A wanderer over the plain,
I am the soul of color,
I am the Iris of rain.

Enchantress of water and fire,
Where I pass in a radiant hour,
The tree-tops mist into verdure,
The meadows spring into flower.

I am the iridescence
Hid in the bowl of glass;
The glamour of light and shadow,
The glory of things that pass.

I rim the far horizon
With magic of melting hues;
I spill on the painted desert
My yellows and roses and blues.

I am the shine and sparkle
Where combers break and flee
In beryl and jade and azure, —
The glitter and gloom of the sea.

I dance on the dazzling snow-drift,
I flash in the quick sunshower,
I am the halo of joyance,
I am the jewel of power.

I reign o'er the fairy ice-storm,

Preside over winter's dream,
To color his pallid splendor
With magical fire and gleam.

I burn in the heart of the opal,
I melt in the sphere of the dew,
I sleep on the lake's still mirror,
I lurk in the icy blue.

When the feet of the legions of thunder
And the spears of the lightning have passed
Through the echoing gates of the mountains,
Shadowy, threatening, and vast,

I rise undefeated behind them,
As only the rapturous can,
And spring for a signal of triumph
My arch of the airy span.

Lights which have been playing about **IRIS** during this scene form a rainbow as she disappears to the left.

THE STUDENT
So earth is held in expectant trance,—
Enchanted by sheer radiance.

Hark! Hath the silence not a call?
Out of the low wind's lift and fall,

Wonder emerges in throb and tone
With transport of meaning,—music's own.

My heart is made like a cunning shell
Where answering echoes wake and dwell,

Interpreting the rhythm and cry
Of every beauty passing by.

O mystic life of this lovely morn,
How is thy magic of music born?

SYRINX is disclosed in a clump of reeds at the left, and **THE STUDENT** drops upon one knee before her.

SYRINX
I am Syrinx, soul of the reed.
In me the music of earth is freed.

The immortal cadence all men know
Lurks at my lip; but a god must blow.

Since first I was found and wooed by Pan,
I have taught the rhythm of life to man.

In the flush of dawn when the meadows gleam,
I flute for joy to the wandering stream,

Till the thrushes open their golden throats
To echo the thrill of my reedy notes.

The grass-heads bend and the branches sway,
And the traveller lingers beside the way,

As I turn my lilt with the dying fall,
And the field-lark answers my eerie call.

When only the dry cicada sings,
And the sultry locust claps his wings,

In the languorous heat I drowse and swoon
At the burning touch of the dreaming noon,

Or swing with the sailing wind and sigh
For the pageant of summer passing by.

When the full moon rises frail and large,
And shadows steal from the wooded marge,

In many a valley I answer the drone
Of little rivers lost and lone,

Till my head is bowed and I rock with them
Under the Twilight's purple hem,

Where all tunes out of the ancient heart,—
Sorrow and longing and love,—are part

Of the infinite music made for man
By a breath of life and the flute of Pan.

SYRINX disappears through the woods to the left, piping, while **THE STUDENT** rises as if to follow her.

THE STUDENT
Immortal music, turn not yet!
With grateful tears my eyes are wet

For that sheer loveliness of thine,
The pure cool touch of the tone divine.

(A wild **RABBIT** crosses the scene.)

See how the wild things haste to hear
The call of rapture that knows no fear!

O creatures with eyes as clear as dew,
Is there a heart that cares for you,

Beating somewhere within the wild
With fostering love for a feckless child,—

An all-kind mother, as men suppose,
Ready with solace for all our woes?

FAUNA comes quickly upon the scene from the left holding back a large white wolfhound. **THE STUDENT** approaches, extending a friendly hand to them.

FAUNA
Men call me kind, because I know
The needs of all who come and go.

All living creatures of the earth,
Sorry and glad, are mine from birth,

To guard by night, to guide by day,
To cherish in their guileless play.

I give them strength, and make them free
In impulse and in symmetry.

My life throbs with them, as the tide
Throbs in the ocean's heaving side.

Like wind we wander as we will,
By watered plain or shadowy hill.

From craggy peak to sounding coast
Range Fauna and her teeming host.

(She sets free the **DOG**.)

The timid doe, the startled hare,
Flee or lie hidden in my care.

When all the swampy barrens ring
With the first chorus of the spring,

It is my voice that sounds the note
For every wild inflated throat.

When the first swallow skims the blue,
It is my smile he answers to.

The wild hawk wheeling ring on ring,
Poised as I taught on tilted wing

Above the perilous ravine,
Mounts to his pinnacle unseen.

The dragon-fly along the stream
Moves like a shuttle through my dream.

The lumbering bear that roves the wood
Includes me in his solitude.

The squirrel on the bending spray
Leaps, and is gone my leafy way.

My young fox clears the orchard wall
As lightly as a thistle-ball.

Through magic dusks on moonlit lawns.
I frolic with my dancing fauns.

But first of all my tribes I place
The man-cub with his laughing face.

Like a young wood-god starry-eyed
He moves before me in his pride.

Subduer of the land and sea,
He leads life's wondrous pageantry,

Till I behold him pass from sight
Through the mysterious door of night;

And I who all his joys have known,
Am left here by his altar stone,

While sorrow with the long gray rain
Settles upon the darkening plain.

THE STUDENT stands with head bowed down, while **FAUNA** quickly vanishes to the right.

THE STUDENT

Ah, what is man? What power ordains
The unresting impulse in his veins,

Which drives him on from hope to hope
Through time's immeasurable scope?

A spirit radiant as day,
Illumining its house of clay,

With an unquenchable desire
That must forevermore aspire!

The wind that lifts the dust of spring
And makes the murmuring pines to sing,

Blowing o'er every land and sea
Is not more glad of being free.

PSYCHE appears on the rising ground above the altar, slowly moving down. THE STUDENT speaks the lines that follow.

PSYCHE
Tender as wind of summer
That wanders among the flowers,
Down worldly aisles with enchanted smiles
She leads the mysterious hours.

This is immortal Psyche,
The winged soul of man, —
Ardor unspent and innocent
As when the world began.

Out of the ancient silence
Over the darkling earth,
As streamers swim on the sunrise rim,
She moves between sorrow and mirth.

The impulse of things eternal,
The transport hidden in clay,
Like a dancing beam on a noonday stream,
She signals along the way.

Her feet are poised over peril,
Her eyes are familiar with death,
Her radiant wings are daring things,
Frail as the beat of a breath.

Over the ocean of being,

In her gay incredible flight,
See her float and run in the gold of the sun,
Down to the gates of night.

The storm may darken above her,
The surges thunder below,
But on through a rift where the gold lights drift,
Still she will dancing go,

Treasuring things forgotten,
As dreams and destinies fade;
Spirit of truth and ageless youth,
She laughs and is not afraid.

(She dances off to the left.)

THE STUDENT
Surely, far off on the morning's verge,
I hear the great sea thunder and surge!

In a lull of the wind that wanders by
I hear the haunting and eerie cry

Of the wild white riders of the foam
And the sound of their coursers trampling home.

O dancing joy of the might of the sea,
Wilt thou not for once take form for me,

And flash from the spray and the flying spume
That rides on the slope of the beryl gloom,

When the breaking billows hiss and roar,
And the daring combers race for shore!

BEROE springs upon the scene from the right.

A solo **VOICE** and chorus off scene.

BEROE
Beroe, daughter of Ocean,
Foam of the wave is she!
On the crest of the racing billows
Shoreward her white feet flee.

Crowding, breaking, and tossing,
Her cloud-white stallions run,
While poised on their curving shoulders

See her dance in the dazzling sun!

Glad, glad to the open heaven,
On the track of the coursing tides,
To the sound of their trampled thunder
With their flying manes she rides.

The slope of the beach is before them,
The hurrying legions behind,
But her hands are light on the bridle,
Her feet are soft as the wind.

Up, up on the far-flung shingle
To the edge of the dunes they go,
To pause for a melting moment
And swirl like a wraith of snow.

Then back for the slow recover
Their shattered charge recedes,
And she passes the gates of sundown,
On the necks of her plunging steeds.

She dances off to the right.

THE STUDENT
O sea-soul, follow your restless tides,—
While peace in the bosom of earth abides!

(He seats himself on a fallen tree.)

From the pointed firs on the western hill
Our earth-born farewells follow you still.

Now the sun-warm wind from a harvest field
Comes with the breath of the fragrant yield,

Is it the sheen of glimmering feet
That runs on the crests of the rippling wheat?

Where is the fervour heroic born
That guards the youth of the standing corn,

And brings its trophies when all is o'er
Without regret to the threshing floor?

CERES walks on from the left surrounded by a glory of sunlight. **THE STUDENT** slips to a kneeling posture before her.

CERES

I am the daughter of earth and sun;
In the dusk I dream; in the wind I run.

I touch the fields with a greening fire,
And the yellow harvest is my desire.

When over hill comes the silver rain,
I spring with joy of the springing grain.

The farmlands love me, the acres know
Promise and fragrance where I go.

Over the furrows I wave my hand,
And gladness walks through the plenteous land.

Through all the valleys at golden morn
My garments sweep with the rustling corn.

The laughing meadows from hill to sea
For a thousand years have been glad of me.

And never came home a harvest load
That passed not Ceres upon the road.

When billows run in the surging rye,
I race with their shadows against the sky,

Lifting the song of the mother kind;
And the scarlet poppies troop behind.

Then when the far-spent rivers croon
To the rising shield of the harvest moon,

With all the good well won from harm
I come at last to the reaper's arm,—

I sink to the ground, my senses dim,
And I give my life for a gift to him.

She walks away to the right, leaving **THE STUDENT** *with bowed head.*

THE STUDENT

Lightly we value the gifts of Earth,
And the things that perish to give life worth!

For every sheaf in the wheatfield lies
Spent in magnanimous sacrifice.

The great unsorrowing sun shines on;
The young grass springs where the scythe has gone;

The redolent air is sweet and bland,
As the rivers sing through the quiet land.

The vineyards slope to the sunburnt hill,
And the clustered grapes hang full and still,

Where soon the gatherers will appear
To crown with rejoicing the yield of the year.

Music is heard from the hill. **THE STUDENT**, listening and looking far off toward the hill, speaks the lines that follow.

Bacchus!... Bacchus!... Bacchus!... Bacchus!

Hark to the drums!
Hark to the drums!
The dance of the lord of the vintage comes.
Out of the wood and down the hill
The rioters follow with rapture shrill.

Youth and maid
In that mad parade
Leap for joy in the flickering shade.
The strongest reel, and the weak grow wan,
And the maddest maenad leads them on.

Her heart is bare,
Her loosened hair
Is a mist of gold on the violet air.
Beauty aflame, she marches by,
Child of the thyrsus borne on high.

Her eyes a-shine,
She is half divine
With the rhythmic dance and the mystic wine;
While the grapes upheld in her gleaming hand
Are an ensign of mirth to her reckless band.

Living as fire
No time can tire,
Or a scarlet lily's unshamed desire,
Her wine-hued mouth and ivory knees
Flash in her sunlit ecstasies.

Trembling clear
As a joyous fear,
The soft insidious flutes draw near;
While madder, madder, madder comes
The frensied throb of the choric drums.

The call of the crowd
Is fond and loud,
As she tosses before them wild and proud.
"Faster, faster, faster," they cry,
As the god with a ravishing smile goes by.

Bacchus!... Bacchus!... Bacchus!... Bacchus!

BACCHANTE and **THE STUDENT** moves up scene where a crowd of revellers rushing past bear him off, while **BACCHANTE** dances on scene, decorates the altar, and dances off to the right as the student returns.

THE STUDENT
Spirit of all the grape-hung South,
With the kiss of the world on thy wilful mouth,

Whose gladness moves in our veins like fire
Unleashing the soul to her dear desire,—

Pass, wild dancer, but leave behind
The pattern of joy for our feet to find!

Thy sister spirit breathes her balm
From Northern orchards mellow and calm,

Where temperate airs make strong and good
The life that rises in sap and blood,

And spreads the bounty of her hand
Over the tranquil autumn land.

POMONA enters from the left.

POMONA
Now my festival is here,
Harvest sun and hunter's cheer,

I Pomona make my round
Of each fruit-lit orchard ground,

Bidding for my dance draw near
Every fruit-stained harvester.

A chorus of **HARVESTERS** enter, carrying fruits, pipes, and cymbals, dancing and singing.

Where like lamps the apples hang
Gay with autumn's tinge and tang,

Here the patterned maze we tread,
Through the shade by color led.

Ruddy tint, through every vein
Carry the patrician strain,

Till each cheek shall wear the sign
Of its origin divine.

Golden glow of molten sun
Caught in globes the year has spun,

Spread the glory of thy spell,
That the land may love thee well!

Darkening tent of royal blue
With the pale stars peeping through,

Shed new wisdom for the wise
From your sky-brewed sorceries!

Exeunt **HARVESTERS**. **POMONA** continues.

Now the pipes and cymbals fade
With the dancers down the glade.

Still the loitering sun delays,
And I linger by the ways,

Dreaming, while the crickets sing,
Of Vertumnus and the spring.

She walks away to the left, where a large white moon is seen. The sun is going down to the right.

THE STUDENT
Spirits of the dreamful earth,
Celebrants at beauty's birth,

Ministering to the sight
Of the seekers of the light,

Marshalling for the sun's eye

His diurnal pageantry,—

Visions, how ye still endure
To inspire and allure!

And upon the brink of night,
Hark, what footsteps fleet and light,—

The summer woodland's fairest child,
The blushing spirit of the wild!

DAPHNE is seen running back and forth among the trees on the hill, and then on to the scene. **THE STUDENT** conceals himself as she approaches. Two following **NYMPHS** appear at the forest's edge and speak.

DAPHNE
Through the shadowy aisles she flees
From the ardour of the sun;
Straining throat and trembling knees
Scarce can bear her farther on.

Great Selene, kind and cold,
Hide her in thy silver light
Of enchantment, fold on fold,
Lest she perish in affright!

Mother of the frail in heart,
To thy forest she is come.
Let the tender branches part,
And their twilight take her home.

Let her wilding bed be made.
By a mossy beech-tree bole,
Deep within its healing shade.
Soon, come soon, that saving goal!

Speak, oh, speak the holy ban,
And thy spell about her shed!
Faster reels the darkening span.
Fiercer burns the nameless dread.

Ah, thy breath begins to cool
All her beauty with its balm!
Here beside a darkling pool,
(Like thy beam within its calm,)

She who Daphne was of yore,
Changed by thy mysterious might,

Now is Laurel evermore,
Gleaming through the tranquil night.

She goes off among the trees at the right, the **NYMPHS** following her. **THE STUDENT** reappears,
approaches the stone, bows his head and bends his knee, and sinks upon the step, resting his head
against the altar.

THE STUDENT
What riches out of Nature's day
Cheer the dreamer on his way,

Till his loving heart is bowed
With the memories that crowd!

And he bends a pilgrim knee,
Thankful for felicity,

While his care-freed senses bless
The solace of the wilderness.

Where the town's distractions pale,
Dusk has drawn a silver veil,

And the glamour of the moon
Takes its convert in a swoon, —

Carries him by drowsy streams
To the borderland of dreams.

He falls asleep. **VERTUMNUS** reappears from the left.

VERTUMNUS
From sunset hills to the sunrise sea,
I am the lore and the ecstasy,

The gladdening strength and the urge of things,
Unaged by love of a thousand springs.

The snow-white Foam and the silver Rain,.
The wilding Mother, the bending Grain,

Laurel and Vine and river Reed,
And the Soul of Man, are mine indeed.

I touch them all with greening fire,
And bring them at last to their hearts' desire.

My triumph awaits the harvest moon,

When the grain is ripe and the grass-heads swoon,

Where slumberous poppies nod and burn,
As summer comes to her drowsy turn.

Then all the laboring earth has rest,
And I sink to sleep on Pomona's breast.

As **VERTUMNUS** alludes to each deity, she appears among the trees; **PSYCHE** on the hill above the altar; to the right from back to front **CERES, DAPHNE, BACCHANTE** and **BEROE**; and to the left **IRIS, FAUNA, SYRINX,** —leaving the front place for **POMONA** who enters before the last couplet. **VERTUMNUS** goes to meet her, and they all assume statuesque poses. The scene is gradually darkened and the figures disappear. **THE STUDENT** wakes and prepares to continue his journey. Dawn lights grow, while he is speaking, until one shaft falls upon the altar.

THE STUDENT
Where are my dreams of beauty gone?
This air, this wood, this very stone—

The same, yet not the same! I see
Them now as masks of deity.

There is a friendliness of light
About them new and infinite;

And they will nevermore appear
The allen common things they were.

Another day! The silent sun
Kindles the clod it falls upon

With ecstasy, and life renews
Itself for its eternal use.

And now for me henceforth, behold
A world that is not as of old!

In every face I shall descry
Some glimpses of divinity.

The laundry girl with bare white throat
And lyric step, and hair aftoat,

Is Beroe, who comes to bless
The town with her fresh loveliness.

The shabby model's perfect face
Smiles on with Ceres' generous grace.

One voice with its caressing tone
Wild, soft, and sad, is Syrinx' own.

Old Apple Mary at her stall
Is not her dingy self at all,

But great Pomona in disguise.
And the old dame with earth-brown eyes

Who tends the bird-shop, with its shelf
Of injured ones, is Fauna's self.

The grapes upon the fruiterer's stand
Were tended by Bacchante's hand.

O world of dusk where dreams are born,
To grow to wisdom with the morn!.

Our visions pass, but their truth remains.
So man aspires and attains....

Back by the green and shadowy road
To carry the news from the gods' abode!

O sun be with me along the way,
And spread thy glamour through town to-day,

That folk in the dreariest plight may see
Some kind revelation of deity!

CURTAIN

CHILDREN OF THE YEAR

PERSONS IN THE MASQUE
MOTHER EARTH
THE TWELVE MONTHS
THEIR TWELVE ESCORTS
TIME, a silent figure.
Overture with bells and chimes in celebration of the new year.

The curtain rises on a wild place among the hills in starlight. A stronger white light centres about a symbolistic figure of **MOTHER EARTH**, who is seated with the **MAIDEN JANUARY** in her embrace.

Each Month in turn, as she is introduced, enters and holds the stage with characteristic motion, (pantomime, and dance,) to appropriate music, to which the lines are sung. She then takes her place on the stage near **EARTH** and joins in the succeeding singing.

Each Month radiates her own peculiar light and atmosphere upon her scene.

MOTHER EARTH
Here's young January,
As fresh as a fairy,
As wondering shy as a child that is lost.
With bells on her sleigh,
She has come a long way,
And her kind-hearted nurse is old lady Frost.

You are welcome, my dear!
The music you hear,
Is folk celebrating the day of your birth.
Your sister months greet you,
And hasten to meet you,
As you stand at the knee of your fond Mother Earth.

FEBRUARY
Here's February coming
Through the crystal-coated trees;
Her cloak is fringed with icicles
That clink about her knees;
She is young and debonair,
With snowdust in her hair,
A-flashing by on silver skates
Or on her winged skis.

Her roads are all unbroken,
Her woods are in a trance,
But there's mischief in her laughter,
And daring in her glance.
This saucy Miss of mine
Has seen her Valentine,
And they will lead the carnival
With domino and dance.
The drifts are in the meadow,
The snow is on the hill,
Along the waiting valleys
The days are white and still.
But a smile is on her lip,
As the eaves begin to drip,
For soon the Harlequin of Spring
Will peep across her sill.

MARCH

Now here comes blowsy March,
With petticoats a-starch,
A-hurrying to market through the mud, mud, mud.
She bears a peck of dust,
Wears a veil of icy crust,
And all the sugar maples are in bud, bud, bud.

She travels with a gale
That goes roaring in the sail,
And sets the wires singing in the blow, blow, blow.
The noons are almost warm,
There is not a sign of storm,
And then in half an hour comes the snow, snow, snow.

You may hear the melting rain
At midnight on the pane,
Then down will go the mercury to freeze, freeze, freeze.

And when up comes the sun
To see what has been done,
He finds a shower of diamonds on the trees, trees, trees.

Then all about the town
There are people falling down,
Until the glary streets are turned to slush, slush, slush.

When all the winds grow still
Along the misty hill,
You're sure to hear a bluebird through the hush, hush, hush.

APRIL

Shining, shining April,
With the merry mouth!
When the sighing rain-wind
Sets from the south,
A light is on her brow,
And a tear is on her cheek,
While with sun and showers
She plays at hide and seek.

Shining, shining April,
With the shadow eyes,
Eager with compassion,
Melting with surprise.
Twilight soft about her,
Violets on her breast,
Welcomed at each open door

As a radiant guest.

Shining, shining April,
With the woodland voice,
Bidding all the rivers
And the hills rejoice.
Every living creature
Wakens at her call,—
Who is not in love with her
Who comes with love for all?

MAY

This is May coming now,
With the blushing apple bough;
And her swallows skim and circle
Where the heavy oxen plow.

When the hurdy-gurdies play,
You may know that it is May
With all her budding comrades.
A-trooping up this way.

There's a sound of marching drums
In the village when she comes,
The lilacs break in blossom
And every beehive hums.

She is willowy and blonde,
She is whimsical and fond,
And rules her willing subjects
With a wilful fairy wand.

Beneath a chilly sky
There is fervor in her eye.
Though she has a changeful temper,
That will better bye-and-bye.

When she dances with a lad,
Her beauty drives him mad,
And when she trips adown the street
The old folks all are glad.

JUNE

This is June, glory-eyed,
Very gracious in her pride,
And how fair!
Through the scented dusk she goes,
With a single yellow rose

In her hair.

And every garden ground,
Where she makes her happy round
Hour by hour,
Is glad of her caress
And her twilight hands that bless
Every flower.

She loiters by the stream,
Where the idle rushes dream
Time away.
As she bends and turns her face,
They imitate her grace,
As they sway.

When she hears her minstrel thrush
Through the purple evening hush,
Hearts unfold.
As she drops her veil of dew,
Romance is shining through,
Still untold.

JULY
This is opulent July,
And as she passes by,
There is triumph in her bearing
And bewitchment in her eye.

There is freedom in her style,
And adventure in her smile;
She travels with the roving bees
O'er many a sunny mile.

From the mountains to the shore,
She has lovers by the score;
Every summer they are captured
By her beauty as of yore.

See her saunter down the beach,
Just beyond the breakers' reach,
With the figure of a sea-nymph
And the color of a peach.

See her standing on a ledge
At a mountain's dizzy edge,
Or following a river
With the iris and the sedge.

A month is like a day
In the glamour of her sway,
And every heart goes singing
Down her green enchanted way.

AUGUST

This is tawny August,
She who wanders by,
Where the hot cicada
Shrills his dusty cry.

Trailing misty garments
Through the sultry land,
With a swinging censer
In her languorous hand;

Slow of foot she passes
Down the village street,
Where the tiger-lilies
Slumber in the heat.

But the eager children
Spy her passing there,
With a scarlet poppy
In her golden hair;

And they troop behind her,
Till a place is found
Where the shade is dancing
Patterns on the ground.

Homeward then she leads them,
Touched with dreams anew,
Through the trance of evening
And her drenching dew.

SEPTEMBER

September is a lady
Of fine patrician mien,
Her gown is harvest yellow,
Her cloak is apple green.

And when she comes a-walking
Serenely from the west,
The clover's to her shoe-top,
The wheat is to her breast;

The corn in tasselled plenty
Is higher than her chin;
They vie with one another
To be her next of kin.

She smiles on little Clover,
She bows to stately Corn,
And signals waving Wheat-ear
Across the rosy morn.

She halts beside the orchard
To watch the squirrels play,
And with the idling sunlight
She tarries on the way.

The sky is clear above her;
But when she turns to go,
From somewhere in the mountains
The storms begin to blow.

OCTOBER

October is a gipsy girl
With hair a-blow and cheek of tan,
Who at the sign of frost appears
With her gay-colored caravan.

The thin blue smoke of morn reveals
Her camp-fire in the distant hills;
At noon she climbs the wooded slope
Or lingers by the cider mills.

In tattered gold and faded red,
She bears her beauty like a queen;
And lonely valleys hear afar
The sounding of her tambourine.

It is the song of rocky streams
Through frosty groves of beech and fir;
It is the dance of yellow leaves
That whirl a tarantelle with her.

Along the road where she must wend
The sumacs with their torches run,
And overhead the crimson oaks
Are gorgeous tents against the sun.

And when she turns a breathless face
To where the cold blue mountains stand,

Lo, Twilight drops a young new moon
Like minted silver in her hand.

NOVEMBER
November, a Puritan maiden,
Is sober in white and grey;
But her quiet wear has a high-bred air,
Her heart is dreamful and gay.

Veiled in the grey of snow-clouds,
Gowned in the grey of trees,
With cap as white as a frosty night
And step like a rising breeze,

She mellows the fruits of the garden,
She treasures the strength of the vine,
And all the worth of the yield of the earth
She sweetens with power benign.

She battles with wind and weather,
She cheers the denuded ranks
Of branches bare to the wintry air,
And for vigor of life gives thanks.

She hears in the starry midnight
The honking geese go by,
And her spirit is stirred by that warning word
Of the journey across the sky.

Then as the great storms gather
And shrieking winds arise,
There's a breath of prayer on the freezing air,
And a love-light in her eyes.

DECEMBER (Disguised as an old woman)
Make way for old December,
Bowed like a shivering crone,
As she scurries down the highway,
Her skirts about her blown.

And huge upon her shoulder,
What means the mighty sack?
It is an inky storm-cloud
She carries on her back.

Ah, see, the sack is leaking!
She's losing half her load,—
A trail of fluttering snowflakes

Swirls all along the road.

They sweep across the common,
And drive along the hill;
They settle in the dooryard
And whiten every sill;

They trim the trees with laces,
The paths are out of sight,
The sagging wires are festooned
Like garlands soft and white.

This is December's witchwork;
And when her task is done,
She will have made a white world
To greet the rising sun.

Hereupon **PRINCE CHARMING** enters and is presented, followed by all the **ESCORTS** of the various months appropriately costumed, who claim their partners and take places to dance, while **EARTH** continues,

And now, January,
Your time to make merry
Is come, and Prince Charming has asked for your hand.
Though youngest of all,
You are belle of the ball,
And shall lead the festivities over the land.

You shall dance through the night,
By the pale Northern Light,
While the stars in a spangled procession go by.
Make merry, my dears,
With the joy of the years;
For gladness abides, though the hours must fly.

At the conclusion of couple dancing ad libitum all join in a symbolistic dance, which is arrested by a rising sun, and the figure of **TIME** appearing. **MOTHER EARTH** announces,

Time passes!

The shrouded figure of **TIME** walks slowly across the background, from right to left; the sun rises; the Months from in line in due order of prededence, **AUGUST** leading, face to the left, and move slowly accross the stage with **TIME**. The youths divide, and fall back right and left, six on each side, taking various prescribed poses of dismay, and holding them, as **JANUARY** reaches centre position in front of **MOTHER EARTH** who sits serenely in her place. Final music is heard in diminishing strains of the dance as Curtain falls.

PERSONS IN THE DANCE
PIERROT
PIERRETTE
COLUMBINE
AN ORGAN-GRINDER

A street scene in spring. An **ORGAN-GRINDER** stands playing in the shade of a tree at the edge of the Common. His music continues throughout the dance, while he himself takes the part of a Chorus.

THE ORGAN-GRINDER
Now Spring is laughing down the street,
With music for her dancing feet,
Tel-oodle-oo, tel-oodle-oo,
Who ever heard, since time began
Of Spring without the organ-man?
Tel-oodle-oo, tel-oodle-oo,
Tel-oodle-ee, tel-oodle!

And here's that vagabond Pierrot,
A-mumming in a suit of woe,
Tel-oodle-oo, tel-oodle-oo,
Whatever can have come his way
To put him out of love to-day?
Tel-oodle-oo, tel-oodle-oo,
Tel-oodle-ee, tel-oodle!

(Enter **PIERROT**)

PIERROT
Ah, love alone,
I ask no more!
I Pierrot!
Though love be mad,
I would adore.

A thousand years
Were not enough
For Pierrot,
If only I
May live in love!

But if this life
No love can give
To Pierrot,
A moment were

Too long to live.

Ah, there is none
To love me now,
And say, "Pierrot,
Why grievest thou?"

White as the moon's
Enchanted fire,
Burned long ago
My soul's desire.

But now all life
Is changed and cold.
There is no joy
As once of old.

There is no hope,
Nor prayer nor vow,
Can save the soul
Of Pierrot now.

Ah, well!
Life still is life,
And hearts are brave,
My Pierrot,
And I may sing
A moonlit stave!

And if my heart
Can mended be,
(Hold, Pierrot!)
I'll sing no more
In mockery.

If love be not
Beyond recall,
(Sst, Pierrot!)
Perhaps the last
Is best of all.

Ah, well! ah, well! ah, well!
Ah, well! ah, well! ah, well!
Ah, well, Pierrot!

(Exit.)

THE ORGAN-GRINDER

O sad is love, and glad is love,
And everlasting mad is love,
Tel-oodle-oo, tel-oodle-oo,
But you must follow, if you can,
The wisdom of the organ-man.
Tel-oodle-ee, tel-oodle!
Tel-oodle-ee, tel-oodle!

There's nothing like the jolly town
In Spring to turn you upside down,
Tel-oodle-oo, tel-oodle-oo,
And make you want to join the clan
That dances for the organ-man.
Tel-oodle-oo, tel-oodle-oo,
Tel-oodle-ee, tel-oodle!

Here comes a saucy little pet,
The glowing gadabout, Pierrette,
Tel-oodle-oo, tel-oodle-oo,
As fresh as tulips in the pan.
O pity the poor old organ-man!
Tel-oodle-oo, tel-oodle-oo,
Tel-oodle-ee, tel-oodle!

(Enter **PIERRETTE**.)

PIERRETTE
The shops are full of gossamers,
The hats are full of flowers,
The clouds that look quite innocent
Are capable of showers.

I feel that I should like to drift
On some adventure new,
In the green world of fairy-land,
Or Cupid's garden blue!

(Exit.)

THE ORGAN-GRINDER
O listen to the music play,
For that can take you far away!
Tel-oodle-oo, tel-oodle-oo,
You do not need a moving van,
You only need the organ-man.
Tel-oodle-oo, tel-oodle-oo,
Tel-oodle-ee, tel-oodle!

For he will play, and you shall be
Transported to Spring mystery.
Tel-oodle-oo, tel-oodle-oo,
It is the universal plan
For moving, says the organ-man.
Tel-oodle-oo, tel-oodle-oo,
Tel-oodle-ee, tel-oodle!

I dance the children.up the street,
I dance the watchman on his beat,
Tel-oodle-oo, tel-oodleoo,
I dance the traveller into town,
I dance away the angry frown,
Tel-oodle-oo, tel-oodle-oo,
Tel-oodle-ee, tel-oodle!

I even dance the sun to shine,
When April comes— and Columbine!
Tel-oodle-oo, tel-oodle-oo,
That blush of roses on her tan
Betrays her to the organ-man.
Tel-oodle-oo, tel-oodle-oo,
Tel-oodle-ee, tel-oodle!

(Enter **COLUMBINE**.)

COLUMBINE
The world is full of lilac now,
A smile is in the sky,
And in my heart a little bird
Is singing B-o-y!

What is there is in the silly song
To set my cheek aglow?
Can it be love that's ailing me?
Pray, master, do you know?

(Exit.)

THE ORGAN-MAN
It can be nothing else, my dear,
When Spring is in the atmosphere,
Tel-oodle-oo, tel-oodle-oo,
You know it only needs the Spring
To make us all to love and sing.
Tel-oodle-oo, tel-oodle-oo,
Tel-oodle-ee, tel-oodle!

Perhaps you never heard of Pan?
He was a kind of organ-man,
Tel-oodle-oo, tel-oodle-oo,
And many a lady in the Spring
Encountered his philandering.
Tel-oodle-oo, tel-oodle-oo,
Tel-oodle-ee, tel-oodle!

There was no nymph about the place,
But he could pipe to his embrace.
Tel-oodle-oo, tel-oodle-oo.
I often wish that I were Pan,
Instead of just an organ-man.
Tel-oodle-oo, tel-oodle-oo,
Tel-oodle-ee, tel-oodle!

Re-enter **PIERROT**, **PIERRETTE**, and **COLUMBINE** from different directions, for their trio dance

THE ORGAN-MAN
Now here comes trouble down the street!
Two sweethearts and one lover meet.
Tel-oodle-oo, tel-oodle-oo.
That never was the heavenly plan
Of peace, opines the organ-man..
Tel-oodle-oo, tel-ooddle-oo,
Tel-oodle-ee, tel-oodle!

First he approaches—Pierrette.
But she is not an angel yet.
Tel-oodle-oo, tel-ooddle-oo.
She will not speak to Columbine,
In whose bright eyes the tear-drops shine.
Tel-oodle, oo, tel-oodle-oo,
Tel-oodle-ee, tel-oodle!

Hoity-toity, what a scene!
Enter the Monster with Eyes of Green!
Tel-oodle-oo, tel-oodle-oo.
Did ever sage or harlequin
Know how to choose or how to win!
Tel-oodle-oo, tel-oodle-oo,
Tel-oodle-ee, tel-oodle!

Alas, that ever loves should be
In such confused proximity!
Tel-oodle-oo, tel-oodle-oo.
"O, be as wary as you can!
One at a time!" says the organ-man.

Tel-oodle-oo, tel-oodle-oo,
Tel-oodle-ee, tel-oodle!

One pulls him this way, one pulls him that,
While his poor heart beats rat-ta-ta-tat.
Tel-oodle-oo, tel-oodle-oo.
Either or neither, when both are so fair,
Is enough to send any man into the air.
Tel-oodle-oo, tel-oodle-oo,
Tel-oodle-ee, tel-oodle!

They all go out in different directions, leaving the **ORGAN-GRINDER** alone.

O, love is a dance to a roundelay!
It may last an hour or last alway.
Tel-oodle-oo, tel-oodle-oo,
But how it will end, or how it began,
You never can tell, says the organ-man.
Tel-oodle-oo, tel-oodle-oo, —

The music is broken off abruptly as the ORGAN-GRINDER moves on.

NOTE

The following suggestions for the costumes of the Months and their escorts may be of service in amateur presentations of the Children of The Year, and of course may be modified or changed considerably at will.

THE MONTHS
JANUARY - White chiffon.
FEBRUARY - White net with crystal and gold spangles.
MARCH - Cold sky-blue with cloud grey, mousseline de sole.
APRIL - Water-blue and pale leaf-green, marquisette.
MAY - Sky-blue and apple-blossom pink and white, chiffon.
JUNE - Yellow and rose liberty silk.
JULY - Shades of green from light to dark, chiffon and soft silk.
AUGUST - Lilac and gold, chiffon and cloth of gold.
SEPTEMBER - Grain-yellow and apple-green, marquisette.
OCTOBER - Indian reds and yellows, voile.
NOVEMBER - Tree grey, chiffon cloth and white organdie.
DECEMBER - White cloth with swan's down, and dark blue-grey chiffon cloak.
EARTH - Shades of brown crepe de chine and chiffon.
TIME - Greys.

THE ESCORTS
JANUARY, Court costume - White and blue velvet
FEBRUARY, Harlequin - Greenish gold
MARCH, Midshipman - Navy blue

APRIL, Minstrel - Green velvet and white
MAY, Country Boy - Brown cloth and white
JUNE, Artist - Black velvet and soft shirt
JULY, Tennis Player - White flannels
AUGUST, Yachtsman - Navy blue and white
SEPTEMBER, Tramping costume - Tans and brown
OCTOBER, Gipsy - Purple and tan
NOVEMBER, Puritan - Grey and white
DECEMBER, Skater - Red and white

In case it is desirable to adapt the Masque to a larger company of players, each Month may be attended by a number of comrades in suitable characters, as follows:

FEBRUARY - A group of carnival merry-makers.
MARCH - A group of Winds.
APRIL - Spirits of Sun and Rain.
MAY - The Spring flowers, dandelion, apple-blossom, plum-blossom, etc.
JUNE - Roses of many varieties.
JULY - Sea nymphs and wood nymphs.
AUGUST - A company of Picnickers.
SEPTEMBER - Clover, Corn, Wheat, and Fruits.
OCTOBER - A company of Gipsies.
NOVEMBER - Spirits of the Grey Trees.
DECEMBER - Snow Fairies.
JANUARY - Prince Charming alone.

Bliss Carman - An Appreciation

How many Canadians—how many even among the few who seek to keep themselves informed of the best in contemporary literature, who are ever on the alert for the new voices—realise, or even suspect, that this Northern land of theirs has produced a poet of whom it may be affirmed with confidence and assurance that he is of the great succession of English poets? Yet such—strange and unbelievable though it may seem—is in very truth the case, that poet being (to give him his full name) William Bliss Carman. Canada has full right to be proud of her poets, a small body though they are; but not only does Mr. Carman stand high and clear above them all—his place (and time cannot but confirm and justify the assertion) is among those men whose poetry is the shining glory of that great English literature which is our common heritage.

If any should ask why, if what has been just said is so, there has been—as must be admitted—no general recognition of the fact in the poet's home land, I would answer that there are various and plausible, if not good, reasons for it.

First of all, the poet, as thousands more of our young men of ambition and confidence have done, went early to the United States, and until recently, except for rare and brief visits to his old home down by the sea, has never returned to Canada—though for all that, I am able to state, on his own authority, he is still a Canadian citizen. Then all his books have had their original publication in the United States, and while a few of them have subsequently carried the imprints of Canadian publishers, none of these can be said ever to have made any special effort to push their sale. Another reason for the fact above mentioned is that Mr. Carman has always scorned to advertise himself, while his work has never been the subject of the log-rolling and booming which the work of many another poet has had—to his ultimate loss. A further reason is that he follows a rule of his own in preparing his books for publication. Most poets publish a volume of their work as soon as, through their industry and perseverance, they have material enough on hand to make publication desirable in their eyes. Not so with Mr. Carman, however, his rule being not to publish until he has done sufficient work of a certain general character or key to make a volume. As a result, you cannot fully know or estimate his work by one book, or two books, or even half a dozen; you must possess or be familiar with every one of the score and more volumes which contain his output of poetry before you can realise how great and how many-sided is his genius.

It is a common remark on the part of those who respond readily to the vigorous work of Kipling, or Masefield, even our own Service, that Bliss Carman's poetry has no relation to or concern with ordinary, everyday life. One would suppose that most persons who cared for poetry at all turned to it as a relief from or counter to the burdens and vexations of the daily round; but in any event, the remark referred to seems to me to indicate either the most casual acquaintance with Mr. Carman's work, or a complete misunderstanding and misapprehension of the meaning of it. I grant that you will find little or nothing in it all to remind you of the grim realities and vexing social problems of this modern existence of ours; but to say or to suggest that these things do not exist for Mr. Carman is to say or to suggest something which is the reverse of true. The truth is, he is aware of them as only one with the sensitive organism of a poet can be; but he does not feel that he has a call or mission to remedy them, and still less to sing of them. He therefore leaves the immediate problems of the day to those who choose, or are led, to occupy themselves therewith, and turns resolutely away to dwell upon those things which for him possess infinitely greater importance.

"What are they?" one who knows Mr. Carman only as, say, a lyrist of spring or as a singer of the delights of vagabondia probably will ask in some wonder. Well, the things which concern him above all, I would answer, are first, and naturally, the beauty and wonder of this world of ours, and next the mystery of the earthly pilgrimage of the human soul out of eternity and back into it again.

The poems in the present volume—which, by the way, can boast the high honor of being the very first regular Canadian edition of his work—will be evidence ample and conclusive to every reader, I am sure, of the place which

The perennial enchanted
Lovely world and all its lore

occupy in the heart and soul of Bliss Carman, as well as of the magical power with which he is able to convey the deep and unfailing satisfaction and delight which they possess for him. They, however, represent his latest period (he has had three well-defined periods), comprising selections from three of his last published volumes: The Rough Rider, Echoes from Vagabondia, and April Airs, together with a number of new poems, and do not show, except here and there and by hints and flashes, how great is his preoccupation with the problem of man's existence—

—the hidden import
Of man's eternal plight.

This is manifest most in certain of his earlier books, for in these he turns and returns to the greatest of all the problems of man almost constantly, probing, with consummate and almost unrivalled use of the art of expression, for the secret which surely, he clearly feels, lies hidden somewhere, to be discovered if one could but pierce deeply enough. Pick up Behind the Arras, and as you turn over page after page you cannot but observe how incessantly the poet's mind—like the minds of his two great masters, Browning and Whitman—works at this problem. In "Behind the Arras," the title poem; "In the Wings," "The Crimson House," "The Lodger," "Beyond the Gamut," "The Juggler"—yes, in every poem in the book—he takes up and handles the strange thing we know as, or call, life, turning it now this way, now that, in an effort to find out its meaning and purpose. He comes but little nearer success in this than do most of the rest of men, of course; but the magical and ever-fresh beauty of his expression, the haunting melody of his lines, the variety of his images and figures and the depth and range of his thought, put his searchings and ponderings in a class by themselves.

Lengthy quotation from Mr. Carman's books is not permitted here, and I must guide myself accordingly, though with reluctance, because I believe that in a study such as this the subject should be allowed to speak for himself as much as possible. In "Behind the Arras" the poet describes the passage from life to death as

A cadence dying down unto its source
In music's course,

and goes on to speak of death as

—the broken rhythm of thought and man,
The sweep and span
Of memory and hope
About the orbit where they still must grope
For wider scope,

To be through thousand springs restored, renewed,
With love imbrued,
With increments of will
Made strong, perceiving unattainment still
From each new skill.

Now follow some verses from "Behind the Gamut," to my mind the poet's greatest single achievement;

As fine sand spread on a disc of silver,
At some chord which bids the motes combine,
Heeding the hidden and reverberant impulse,
Shifts and dances into curve and line,

The round earth, too, haply, like a dust-mote,
Was set whirling her assigned sure way,
Round this little orb of her ecliptic
To some harmony she must obey.

And what of man?

Linked to all his half-accomplished fellows,
Through unfrontiered provinces to range—
Man is but the morning dream of nature,
Roused to some wild cadence weird and strange.

Here, now, are some verses from "Pulvis et Umbra," which is to be found in Mr. Carman's first book, Low Tide on Grand Pré, and in which the poet addresses a moth which a storm has blown into his window:

For man walks the world with mourning
Down to death and leaves no trace,
With the dust upon his forehead,
And the shadow on his face.

Pillared dust and fleeing shadow
As the roadside wind goes by,
And the fourscore years that vanish
In the twinkling of an eye.

"Pillared dust and fleeing shadow." Where in all our English literature will one find the life history of man summed up more briefly and, at the same time, more beautifully, than in that wonderful line? Now follows a companion verse to those just quoted, taken from "Lord of My Heart's Elation," which stands in the forefront of From the Green Book of the Bards. It may be remarked here that while the poet recurs again and again to some favorite thought or idea, it is never in the same words. His expression is always new and fresh, showing how deep and true is his inspiration. Again it is man who is pictured:

A fleet and shadowy column
Of dust and mountain rain,
To walk the earth a moment
And be dissolved again.

But while Mr. Carman's speculations upon life's meaning and the mystery of the future cannot but appeal to the thoughtful-minded, it is as an interpreter of nature that he makes his widest appeal. Bliss Carman, I must say here, and emphatically, is no mere landscape-painter; he never, or scarcely ever, paints a picture of nature for its own sake. He goes beyond the outward aspect of things and interprets or translates for us with less keen senses as only a poet whose feeling for nature is of the deepest and profoundest, who has gone to her whole-heartedly and been taken close to her warm bosom, can do. Is this not evident from these verses from "The Great Return"—originally called "The Pagan's Prayer," and for some inscrutable reason to be found only in the limited Collected Poems, issued in two stately volumes in 1905.

When I have lifted up my heart to thee,
Thou hast ever hearkened and drawn near,
And bowed thy shining face close over me,
Till I could hear thee as the hill-flowers hear.

When I have cried to thee in lonely need,

Being but a child of thine bereft and wrung,
Then all the rivers in the hills gave heed;
And the great hill-winds in thy holy tongue—

That ancient incommunicable speech—
The April stars and autumn sunsets know—
Soothed me and calmed with solace beyond reach
Of human ken, mysterious and low.

Who can read or listen to those moving lines without feeling that Mr. Carman is in very truth a poet of
nature—nay, Nature's own poet? But how could he be other when, in "The Breath of the Reed" (From
the Green Book of the Bards), he makes the appeal?

Make me thy priest, O Mother,
And prophet of thy mood,
With all the forest wonder
Enraptured and imbued.

As becomes such a poet, and particularly a poet whose birth-month is April, Mr. Carman sings much of
the early spring. Again and again he takes up his woodland pipe, and lo! Pan himself and all his train
troop joyously before us. Yet the singer's notes for all his singing never become wearied or strident; his
airs are ever new and fresh; his latest songs are no less spontaneous and winning than were his first,
written how many years ago, while at the same time they have gained in beauty and melody. What
heart will not stir to the vibrant music of his immortal "Spring Song," which was originally published in
the first Songs from Vagabondia, and the opening verses of which follow?

Make me over, mother April,
When the sap begins to stir!
When thy flowery hand delivers
All the mountain-prisoned rivers,
And thy great heart beats and quivers
To revive the days that were,
Make me over, mother April,
When the sap begins to stir!

Take my dust and all my dreaming,
Count my heart-beats one by one,
Send them where the winters perish;
Then some golden noon recherish
And restore them in the sun,
Flower and scent and dust and dreaming,
With their heart-beats every one!

That poem is sufficient in itself to prove that Bliss Carman has full right and title to be called Spring's
own lyrist, though it may be remarked here that not all his spring poems are so unfeignedly joyous.
Many of them indeed, have a touch, or more than a touch, of wistfulness, for the poet knows well that
sorrow lurks under all joy, deep and well hidden though it may be.

Mr. Carman sings equally finely, though perhaps not so frequently, of summer and the other seasons; but as he has other claims upon our attention, I shall forbear to labor the fact, particularly as the following collection demonstrates it sufficiently. One of those other claims is as a writer of sea poetry. Few poets, it may be said, have pictured the majesty and the mystery, the beauty and the terror of the sea, better than he. His Ballads of Lost Haven is a veritable treasure-house for those whose spirits find kinship in wide expanses of moving waters. One of the best known poems in this volume is "The Gravedigger," which opens thus:

Oh, the shambling sea is a sexton old,
And well his work is done.
With an equal grave for lord and knave,
He buries them every one.

Then hoy and rip, with a rolling hip,
He makes for the nearest shore;
And God, who sent him a thousand ship,
Will send him a thousand more;
But some he'll save for a bleaching grave,
And shoulder them in to shore—
Shoulder them in, shoulder them in,
Shoulder them in to shore.

In "The City of the Sea" (Last Songs from Vagabondia) Mr. Carman speaks of the seabells sounding

The eternal cadence of sea sorrow
For Man's lot and immemorial wrong—
The lost strains that haunt the human dwelling
With the ghost of song.

Elsewhere he speaks of

The great sea, mystic and musical.

And here from another poem is a striking picture:

... the old sea
Seems to whimper and deplore
Mourning like a childless crone
With her sorrow left alone—
The eternal human cry
To the heedless passer-by.

I have said above that Mr. Carman has had three distinct periods, and intimated that the poems in the following collection are of his third period. The first period may be said to be represented by the Low Tide and Behind the Arras volumes, while the second is displayed in the three volumes of Songs from Vagabondia, which he published in association with his friend Richard Hovey. Bliss Carman was from the first too original and individual a poet to be directly influenced by anyone else; but there can be no doubt that his friendship with Hovey helped to turn him from over-preoccupation with mysteries which, for all their greatness, are not for man to solve, to an intenser realisation of the beauty and loveliness of the world about him and of the joys of human fellowship. The result is seen in such poems as "Spring Song," quoted in part above, and his perhaps equally well-known "The Joys of the Road," which appeared in the same volume with that poem, and a few verses from which follow:

Now the joys of the road are chiefly these:
A crimson touch on the hardwood trees;

A vagrant's morning wide and blue,
In early fall, when the wind walks, too;

A shadowy highway cool and brown,
Alluring up and enticing down

From rippled waters and dappled swamp,
From purple glory to scarlet pomp;

The outward eye, the quiet will,
And the striding heart from hill to hill.

Some of the finest of arman's work is contained in his elegiac or memorial poems, in which he commemorates Keats, Shelley, William Blake, Lincoln, Stevenson, and other men for whom he has a kindred feeling, and also friends whom he has loved and lost. Listen to these moving lines from "Non Omnis Moriar," written in memory of Gleeson White, and to be found in Last Songs from Vagabondia:

There is a part of me that knows,
Beneath incertitude and fear,
I shall not perish when I pass
Beyond mortality's frontier;

But greatly having joyed and grieved,
Greatly content, shall hear the sigh
Of the strange wind across the lone
Bright lands of taciturnity.

In patience therefore I await
My friend's unchanged benign regard,—
Some April when I too shall be
Spilt water from a broken shard.

In "The White Gull," written for the centenary of the birth of Shelley in 1892, and included in By the Aurelian Wall, he thus apostrophizes that clear and shining spirit:

O captain of the rebel host,
Lead forth and far!
Thy toiling troopers of the night
Press on the unavailing fight;
The sombre field is not yet lost,

With thee for star.

Thy lips have set the hail and haste
Of clarions free
To bugle down the wintry verge
Of time forever, where the surge
Thunders and trembles on a waste
And open sea.

In "A Seamark," a threnody for Robert Louis Stevenson, which appears in the same volume, the poet hails "R.L.S." (of whose tribe he may be said to be truly one) as

The master of the roving kind,

and goes on:

O all you hearts about the world
In whom the truant gypsy blood,
Under the frost of this pale time,
Sleeps like the daring sap and flood
That dreams of April and reprieve!
You whom the haunted vision drives,
Incredulous of home and ease.
Perfection's lovers all your lives!

You whom the wander-spirit loves
To lead by some forgotten clue
Forever vanishing beyond
Horizon brinks forever new;
Our restless loved adventurer,
On secret orders come to him,
Has slipped his cable, cleared the reef,
And melted on the white sea-rim.

"Perfection's lovers all your lives." Of these, it may be said without qualification, is Bliss Carman himself.

No summary of Mr. Carman's work, however cursory, would be worthy of the name if it omitted mention of his ventures in the realm of Greek myth. From the Book of Myths is made up of work of that sort, every poem in it being full of the beauty of phrase and melody of which Mr. Carman alone has the secret. The finest poems in the book, barring the opening one, "Overlord," are "Daphne," "The Dead Faun," "Hylas," and "At Phædra's Tomb," but I can do no more here than name them, for extracts would fail to reveal their full beauty. And beauty, after all is said, is the first and last thing with Mr. Carman. As he says himself somewhere:

The joy of the hand that hews for beauty
Is the dearest solace under the sun.

And again

The eternal slaves of beauty
Are the masters of the world.

A slave—a happy, willing slave—to beauty is the poet himself, and the world can never repay him for
the message of beauty which he has brought it.

Kindred to From the Book of Myths, but much more important, is Sappho: One Hundred Lyrics, one of
the most successful of the numerous attempts which have been made to recapture the poems by that
high priestess of song which remain to us only in fragments. Mr. Carman, as Charles G. D. Roberts
points out in an introduction to the volume, has made no attempt here at translation or paraphrasing;
his venture has been "the most perilous and most alluring in the whole field of poetry"—that of
imaginative and, at the same time, interpretive construction. Brief quotation again would fail to convey
an adequate idea of the exquisiteness of the work, and all I can do, therefore, is to urge all lovers of real
poetry to possess themselves of Sappho: One Hundred Lyrics, for it is literally a storehouse of lyric
beauty.

I must not fail here to speak of From the Book of Valentines, which contains some lovely things, notably
"At the Great Release." This is not only one of the finest of all Mr. Carman's poems, but it is also one of
the finest poems of our time. It is a love poem, and no one possessing any real feeling for poetry can
read it without experiencing that strange thrill of the spirit which only the highest form of poetry can
communicate. "Morning and Evening," "In an Iris Meadow," and "A letter from Lesbos" must be also
mentioned. In the last named poem, Sappho is represented as writing to Gorgo, and expresses herself
in these moving words:

If the high gods in that triumphant time
Have calendared no day for thee to come
Light-hearted to this doorway as of old,
Unmoved I shall behold their pomps go by—
The painted seasons in their pageantry,
The silvery progressions of the moon,
And all their infinite ardors unsubdued,
Pass with the wind replenishing the earth

Incredulous forever I must live
And, once thy lover, without joy behold,
The gradual uncounted years go by,
Sharing the bitterness of all things made.

Mention must be now made of Songs of the Sea Children, which can be described only as a collection of
the sweetest and tenderest love lyrics written in our time—

—the lyric songs
The earthborn children sing,
When wild-wood laughter throngs
The shy bird-throats of spring;
When there's not a joy of the heart
But flies like a flag unfurled,

And the swelling buds bring back
The April of the world.

So perfect and complete are these lyrics that it would be almost sacrilege to quote any of them unless entire. Listen however, to these verses:

The day is lost without thee,
The night has not a star.
Thy going is an empty room
Whose door is left ajar.

Depart: it is the footfall
Of twilight on the hills.
Return: and every rood of ground
Breaks into daffodils.

There are those who will have it that Bliss Carman has been away from Canada so long that he has ceased to be, in a real sense, a Canadian. Such assume rather than know, for a very little study of his work would show them that it is shot through and through with the poet's feeling for the land of his birth. Memories of his childhood and youthful years down by the sea are still fresh in Mr. Carman's mind, and inspire him again and again in his writing. "A Remembrance," at the beginning of the present collection, may be pointed to as a striking instance of this, but proof positive is the volume, Songs from a Northern Garden, for it could have been written only by a Canadian, born and bred, one whose heart and soul thrill to the thought of Canada. I would single out from this volume for special mention as being "Canadian" in the fullest sense "In a Grand Pré Garden," "The Keeper's Silence," "At Home and Abroad," "Killoleet," and "Above the Gaspereau," but have no space to quote from them.

But Mr. Carman is not only a Canadian, he is also a Briton; and evidence of this is his Ode on the Coronation, written on the occasion of the crowning of King Edward VII in 1902. This poem—the very existence of which is hardly known among us—ought to be put in the hands of every child and youth who speaks the English tongue, for no other, I dare maintain—nothing by Kipling, or Newbolt, or any other of our so-called "Imperial singers"—expresses more truly and more movingly the deep feeling of love and reverence which the very thought of England evokes in every son of hers, even though it may never have been his to see her white cliffs rise or to tread her storied ground:

O England, little mother by the sleepless Northern tide,
Having bred so many nations to devotion, trust, and pride,
Very tenderly we turn
With welling hearts that yearn
Still to love you and defend you,—let the sons of men discern
Wherein your right and title, might and majesty, reside.

In concluding this, I greatly fear, lamentably inadequate study, I come to the collection which follows, and which, as intimated above, represents the work of Mr. Carman's latest period. I must say at once that, while I yield to no one in admiration for Low Tide and the other books of that period, or for the work of the second period, as represented by the Songs from Vagabondia volumes, I have no hesitation in declaring that I regard the poet's work of the past few years with even higher admiration. It may not possess the force and vigor of the work which preceded it; but anything seemingly missing in that respect is more than made up for me by increased beauty and clarity of expression. The mysticism—verging, or more than verging, at times on symbolism—which marked his earlier poems, and which hung, as it were, as a veil between them and the reader, has gone, and the poet's thought or theme now lies clearly before us as in a mirror. What—to take a verse from the following pages at random—could be more pellucid, more crystal clear in expression—what indeed, could come closer to that achieving of the impossible at which every real poet must aim—than this from "In Gold Lacquer".

Gold are the great trees overhead,
And gold the leaf-strewn grass,
As though a cloth of gold were spread
To let a seraph pass.
And where the pageant should go by,
Meadow and wood and stream,
The world is all of lacquered gold,
Expectant as a dream.

The poet, happily, has fully recovered from the serious illness which laid him low some two years ago, and which for a time caused his friends and admirers the gravest concern, and so we may look forward hopefully to seeing further volumes of verse come from the press to make certain his name and fame. But if, for any reason, this should not be—which the gods forfend!—Later Poems, I dare affirm, must and will be regarded as the fine flower and crowning achievement of the genius and art of Bliss Carman.

R. H. HATHAWAY.
Toronto, 1921.

Bliss Carman – A Short Biography

William Bliss Carman was born in Fredericton, in New Brunswick on April 15th 1861. 'Bliss' was his mother's maiden name. She was descended from Daniel Bliss of Concord, Massachusetts, who was the great-grandfather to Ralph Waldo Emerson.

Carman was educated at Fredericton Collegiate School. Here, under the influence of the headmaster George Robert Parkin, he gained an appreciation of classical literature and was introduced to the poetry of many of the Pre-Raphaelites especially Dante Gabriel Rossetti and Algernon Charles Swinburne.

From here he graduated to the University of New Brunswick, obtaining his B.A. there in 1881. As is common with so many writers his first published piece was for the University magazine and for Carman that was in 1879.

England now beckoned and he spent a year at Oxford and then the University of Edinburgh (1882–1883). He returned home to Canada to work on his M.A. which he obtained from the University of New Brunswick in 1884.

Tragically his father died in January, 1885, followed by his mother in February of the following year. Carman now enrolled in Harvard University for a year. There he met and was part of a literary circle that included the American poet Richard Hovey, who would become his close friend, and later collaborator, on the successful Vagabondia poetry series. Carman and Hovey were members of the "Visionists" circle along with Herbert Copeland and F. Holland Day, who would later form the Boston publishing firm Copeland & Day and, in turn, launch Vagabondia.

After Harvard Carman briefly returned to Canada, but was back in Boston by February of 1890 saying "Boston is one of the few places where my critical education and tastes could be of any use to me in earning money. New York and London are about the only other places." However, he was unable to find work in Boston but was more successful in New York becoming the literary editor of the semi-religious New York Independent. There he helped Canadian poets get published and introduced them to a wider readership than they could receive in Canada.

However, Carman and work as an editor were not destined for a long career together and he was dismissed in 1892. There followed short stays with Current Literature, Cosmopolitan, The Chap-Book, and The Atlantic Monthly. Whilst these appointments provided the basis for a career and an income he was not suited to their demands. From 1895 he would only work as a contributor to magazines and newspapers whilst he worked on his volumes of poetry.

Carman first published a book of poetry in 1893 with Low Tide on Grand Pré. He had written the title poem in the summer of 1886 and it had (whilst he was still at Harvard) been published in the spring of 1887 by Atlantic Monthly. Despite its critical acceptance there was no Canadian company prepared to publish the volume. When an American company did so it went bankrupt. Life was becoming difficult for the young poet.

The following year was decidedly better. His partnership with Richard Hovey had given birth to Songs of Vagabondia and it was published by their friends at Copeland & Day. It was an immediate success. The young men were delighted at such a reception. It quickly sold out and was re-printed a number of times. Although these re-prints were small (usually 500-1000 copies) they were frequent.

On the back of this success they would write a further three volumes, which in their turn were almost as successful. They quickly became the center of a cult following, especially among students who empathized with the poetry's anti-materialistic themes, its celebration of personal freedom, and its glorification of comradeship."

The success of Songs of Vagabondia prompted the Boston firm, Stone & Kimball, to reissue Low Tide on Grand Pré and to hire Carman as the editor of its literary journal, The Chapbook. This ceased after a year when the company relocated and Carman expressed his desire to remain in Boston.

In 1885 Carman brought out Behind the Arras, a somewhat more serious and philosophical work centered on the premise of a long meditation using the speaker's house and its many rooms as a symbol of life and the choices to be made. However, the idea and its execution did not quite meld.

Signficantly, in 1896, Carman met Mrs Mary Perry King, who rapidly became patron, adviser and sometime lover. She put money in his pocket, and food in his mouth and, when he struck bottom, often repaired his confidence as well as helping to sell the work. She also later became his writing collaborator on two verse dramas.

Mitchell Kennerley, Carman's roommate wrote that, "On the rare occasions they had intimate relations they always advised me of by leaving a bunch of violets — Mary favorite flower — on the pillow of my bed." If her husband, Dr. King, knew of this arrangement he seems not to have objected. He was a great supporter of Carman's career and seemingly his wife's complicated involvement with that.

In 1897 Carman published Ballad of Lost Haven, a collection of poetry about the sea. Its notable poems include the macabre sea shanty, The Gravedigger. The following year, 1898, came By the Aurelian Wall, the title poem itself was an elegy to John Keats and the book a collection of formal elegies.

In 1899 his publisher, Lamson, Wolffe was taken over by the Boston firm of Small, Maynard & Co., who had also acquired the rights to Low Tide on Grand Pré. The copyrights to of his books were now held by one publisher and, in lieu of earnings, Carman took what would ultimately be a disastrous financial stake in the company.

As the century turned Carman was hard at work on what would eventually be a five-volume set of poetry; "Pans Pipes". Pan, the goat-god, was traditionally associated with poetry and the coming together of the earthly and the divine. The five volumes were all published between 1902 – 1905.

The inspiration for this came from Mary who had persuaded Carman to write in both prose and poetry about the ideas of 'unitrinianism.' This drew on the theories of François-Alexandre-Nicolas-Chéri Delsarte and was defined as a strategy of mind-body-spirit harmonization aimed at undoing the physical, psychological, and spiritual damage caused by urban modernity. The definition may be rather woolly but for Carman it resulted in some very fine work across the five-volume series. This shared belief between Mary and Carman created a further bond but did isolate him from his circle of friends.

The excellence of a number of these poems did much to install Carman as the most noted of Canadian Poets and eventually their own Poet Laureate. Among the most often quoted and printed are "The Dead Faun" (from Volume I), "Lord of My Heart's Elation" (Volume II) and many of the erotic poems from Volume III.

In the middle of publication in 1903, Small, Maynard failed and with it went all the assets Carman had tied up in the company.

Carman immediately signed with another Boston publisher, L.C. Page, who would publish seven new books of Carman poetry in this hectic period up to 1905. They released a further three books based on Carman's Transcript columns, and a prose work on Unitrinianism, The Making of Personality, that he'd written with Mary King.

Carman now felt secure enough to pursue his 'dream project,' namely a deluxe edition of his collected poetry to 1903. Page acquired the distribution rights on the condition that the book be sold privately, by subscription. Unfortunately, the demand wasn't there and it failed. Carman was deeply disappointed and lost faith in Page. However, their grip on his copyrights was absolute and sadly no further collected editions were to be published during his lifetime.

By 1904 his income was restricted and the offer to be editor-in-chief of the 10-volume project, The World's Best Poetry, was eagerly accepted.

For Carman perhaps his best years as a poet were now behind him. From 1908 he lived near the Kings' New Canaan, Connecticut, estate, that he named "Sunshine", or in the summer in a cabin in the Catskills, which he called "Moonshine."

With Literary tastes now moving away from what he could provide his income further dwindled and his health started to deteriorate.

In 1912 Carman published the final work in the Vagabondia series. Richard Hovey had died in 1900 and so this last work was purely his. It has a distinct elegiac tone as if remembering the past works themselves.

Although Carman was not politically active he did campaign during the World War One, as a member of the Vigilantes, who supported the American entry into the titanic struggle on the Allied side.

By 1920, Carman was impoverished and recovering from a near-fatal attack of tuberculosis. He returned to Canada and began to undertake a series of publicly successful and somewhat lucrative reading tours, saying "there is nothing worth talking of in book sales compared with reading. Breathless attention, crowded halls, and a strange, profound enthusiasm such as I never guessed could be,' he reported to a friend. 'And good thrifty money too. Think of it! An entirely new life for me, and I am the most surprised person in Canada.'"

On October 28th, 1921 Carman was honored at a dinner held by the newly-formed Canadian Authors' Association, at the Ritz Carlton Hotel in Montreal, where he was crowned Canada's Poet Laureate with a wreath of maple leaves.

Carman is placed among the Confederation Poets, a group that included his cousin, Charles G.D. Roberts, Archibald Lampman, and Duncan Campbell Scott. Carman was perhaps the best and is credited with the widest recognition. However, whilst the others carefully supplemented their income with writing novels and works for the magazines, or even other careers, Carman only wrote poetry together with a small amount of writing on literary ideas, philosophy, and aesthetics.

He continued his reading tours, and by 1925 had finally secured a new Canadian publisher; McClelland & Stewart (Toronto), who issued a collection of selected earlier verse and would now became his main publisher. Although they benefited from Carman's increased popularity and his revered position in Canadian literature, his former publisher L.C. Page would not relinquish its copyrights to his earlier works.

In his last years, Carman was a member of the Halifax literary and social set, The Song Fishermen and in 1927 he edited The Oxford Book of American Verse.

William Bliss Carman died of a brain hemorrhage, at the age of 68, in New Canaan on the 8th June, 1929. He was cremated in New Canaan and his ashes interred at Forest Hill Cemetery, Fredericton, with a national memorial service held at the Anglican cathedral there.

It was only a quarter of a century later, on May 13th, 1954, that a scarlet maple tree was planted at his graveside, to honour his request in the 1892 poem "The Grave-Tree":

Let me have a scarlet maple
For the grave-tree at my head,
With the quiet sun behind it,
In the years when I am dead.

Poetry Collections
Low Tide on Grand Pre: A Book of Lyrics (1893)
Songs from Vagabondia (1894)
A Seamark: A Threnody for Robert Louis Stevenson (1895)
Behind the Arras: A Book of the Unseen (1895)
More Songs from Vagabondia (1896)
Ballads of Lost Haven: A Book of the Sea (1897)
By the Aurelian Wall: And Other Elegies (1898)
A Winter Holiday (1899)
Last Songs from Vagabondia (1901)
Ballads and Lyrics (1902)
Ode on the Coronation of King Edward (1902)
Pipes of Pan: From the Book of Myths (1902)
Pipes of Pan: From the Green Book of the Bards (1903)
Pipes of Pan: Songs of the Sea Children (1904)
Pipes of Pan: Songs from a Northern Garden (1904)
Pipes of Pan: From the Book of Valentines (1905)
Sappho: One Hundred Lyrics (1904)
Poems (1905)
The Rough Rider: And Other Poems (1909)
A Painter's Holiday, and Other Poems (1911)
Echoes from Vagabondia (1912)
April Airs: A Book of New England Lyrics (1916)
The Man of The Marne: And Other Poems (1918)
The Vengeance of Noel Brassard: A Tale of the Acadian Expulsion (1919)
Far Horizons (1925)
Later Poems (1926)
Sanctuary: Sunshine House Sonnets (1929)
Wild Garden (1929)
Bliss Carman's Poems (1931)

Drama
Bliss Carman & Mary Perry King. Daughters of Dawn: A Lyrical Pageant of a Series of Historical Scenes for Presentation with Music and Dancing (1913)
Bliss Carman & Mary Perry King. Earth Deities: And Other Rhythmic Masques (1914)

Prose Collections
The Kinship of Nature (1904)
The Poetry of Life (1905)
The Friendship of Art (1908)
The Making of Personality (1908)

Talks on Poetry and Life; Being a Series of Five Lectures Delivered Before the University of Toronto, December 1925 (Speech). transcribed by Blanche Hume. 1926.
Bliss Carman's Scrap-Book: A Table of Contents (Pierce, Lorne, editor) (1931)

Editor
The World's Best Poetry (10 volumes) (1904)
The Oxford Book of American Verse (U.S. editor) (1927)
Carman, Bliss; Pierce, Lorne, editors (1935). Our Canadian Literature: Representative Verse, English and French.